CALL AND RESPONSE

CALL AND RESPONSE
Litanies for Congregational Prayer

Fran Pratt

Foreward by Fred Harrell

Table of contents continues on the following page.

It is our joy and privilege to receive people into our community who have little to no experience with a more intentional liturgy. I say 'more intentional' because we are, as James K.A. Smith has said, liturgical animals. Every church has liturgy, but naming it, and intentionally living into it with thoughtfulness and care, is a different experience. My own background in evangelicalism created a liturgical vacuum that made me hungry for something more, I just didn't know what. It was in the discovering of liturgy within my own tradition, combined with discovering similar liturgies outside my tradition, that my soul felt like it was being fed the food for which it was longing.

However, intentional liturgical forms are not merely a recitation of the past, but an ongoing work of the Spirit in the present. Being formed and rooted by ancient liturgies of the past enable creativity in the present. Starting a church in San Francisco 22 years ago was my chance to begin to apply this, and Fran Pratt is doing the same thing. She has been beautifully formed in ancient rituals and practices that, melding with her own creative genius, give way to creative new liturgies, prayers, and songs that cut new grooves into our soul, enable deep longings to find vocabulary for present day expression, and ultimately provide an outlet for a more holistic spiritual formation.

I am so glad Fran Pratt wandered into our church one Sunday years ago. She was an immediate blessing to our community. And now, I am deeply grateful for her contribution to the ongoing 'work of the people'.

Rev. Fred Harrell
Founder and Senior Pastor
City Church San Francisco

I was 28 years old when I first encountered any type of formal liturgy. I had been raised in a conservative evangelical faith environment and then spent years as part of the Vineyard movement. Walking into a liturgical church was like walking into a foreign country. What was this language they were speaking?

This was in 2010. I had just moved with my spouse to San Francisco, and I was five months pregnant with our first daughter when I arrived. It had been a hard couple of years, during which we had left behind a vibrant community in Iowa City, IA where I was a worship leader helping to direct our church's worship ministry. The ministry there had been a source of deep solace for me, and our community and friends there were close-knit and beloved. The churches I grew up in had taught me that what I could do for God was limited because I was a woman. But in Iowa City I had been embraced and empowered and mentored in leadership for six years. I had been trying to follow Jesus since I was a little kid, but for the first time in my life I felt like perhaps I had a calling.

Then in what felt like a flash in early 2009, my spouse's job there was no longer sustainable for him, and we needed to move to find work elsewhere, as I was a graduate student working part-time. What followed was a year of wandering, a year of skirting along the edges of faith, unable to find a home. I was sad and depressed. I'd had a good thing and lost it. I'd had a loving and healthy community and lost it. I'd had a calling, a deep soul-enlivening sense of meaningful work, and was uncertain if I'd ever have it again.

When I walked into the doors of City Church in San Francisco a year later, I didn't know what to think or feel. It was less than a mile walk from our apartment, and they had women pastors - that was all we cared about. I had not one friend in the city. I had no job and no social life. I had never lived in a big city before. The lively faith life I'd had before, and the sense of closeness with Jesus I'd always felt were ghosts I occasionally brushed up against. The creative flow I'd had in music and songwriting was unreachable. About the only scripture I could stomach was the book of Job, and sometimes Lamentations and the darker Psalms. I had not a prayer to pray nor a song to sing.

But an usher handed me a worship guide. I held it in my hands and it was full of prayers, responses, and scriptures, and even a quote for reflection. I didn't have to think about them. I didn't have to conjure up prayers on my own. I could just say them. I could let the words wash over me and not have to do anything but that.

City Church is part of the Reformed Church of America. Their clergy wear collars. When you take communion, someone looks you in the eye and says "The body of Christ broken for you. The blood of Christ shed for you." The cup holds real wine. They follow the Lectionary and the Liturgical Calendar. The music is amazing and the preaching is compelling and done in under a half-hour. It was all new and foreign, a totally different approach to church and faith.

Sometimes I would stand in the very back, with my arms raised and my very pregnant belly protruding, tears running down my face. Because here was some beauty for me to partake of. Here was communion for me to chew and swallow. And here on the page was a prayer that we would all pray aloud together and most often it was prayer disguised as poetry, and more often than not it was the only prayer I'd emitted that week.

We prayed for all kinds of things together: government officials, world crises, the city's homeless population, health, world peace; we observed silences, recited confessions and creeds. I had never encountered such a buffet of spiritual elements. It was a dream-world, but it was a solid rock. Instead of me forming my prayers, I could let the prayers form me.

If I hadn't already been experiencing an identity crisis, then by the time my baby was born and my whole life changed again, I was surely in the midst of one that had rendered myself unrecognizable to me. But I hung on each week to the prayers. I bought a copy of the Book of Common Prayer, and started using it. I kept letting the Lectionary and the liturgy wash over me. And gradually, millimeter by millimeter, I came to be awake again.

Up until then I'd absorbed the idea that the best, holiest kind of praying was done extemporaneously - no one ever said this out loud to me; rather it was communicated by emphasis and practice. You stood up and prayed whatever came to mind. Anything else was lesser, emptier, overly formal and rote. What I couldn't have predicted was how all that rote praying and formal, scheduled reading kept my ship from sinking entirely. Words were not enough to fix me, until somehow they did. And the miracle is this: by the mercy of God I emerged from that loneliness and identity crisis softer-hearted and more compassionate than I was before; the threads of my faith that had felt so frayed before were stronger.

The liturgy had been my midwife. Or rather, the Spirit moving through the liturgy had been to me a midwife. It was present and reliable during a time of numbness mixed with pain and isolation that felt like death; but that, I realized, was more like labor. I remember the moment during my labor at home with my daughter, that transitional moment of clarity when you realize that there is only one way out, and that is *through*. It didn't make any of my pain go away, but it offered me sustenance for the work.

Here, drink this, the liturgy said in that moment.
Eat this for strength.
The Lord be with you.
And also with you.

Some time passed, and another cross-country move, this time to Texas. I was leading worship in a Vineyard church again. And missing the liturgy dearly. So I just decided to be a contemplative on my own. I would lead my modern five-song set, then go home and pray the Psalms and the BCP and write my prayers in my journal, which I'd been doing nearly all my life. They had changed though, taken on more flesh because I had more language to work with. They became less about my own concerns and gradually more broad. So one day, tentatively, I shared a litany I'd written, that we prayed together in church. "What is a litany?" people would ask when I shared what I was doing; "What is this strange thing you're doing?" And from there I kept writing and sharing, and my non-liturgical friends began to catch the spirit and see the value of it, which led to me starting my website in late 2015.

Litany has become for me both spiritual expression, ministry, and artform. It's focused poetry, raised consciousness, and social justice art. It has given me a place to engage with culture and current events, and a place to help congregations and individuals wrestle with hard things. But mostly it's an extension of being with God. Because if I've learned anything about prayer in these years, it's that prayer is more about presence and less about words. It's less about requests and more about formation. The silence of the pause is the best and choicest part. But having a prayer to pray out loud together, like having a song to sing together, can usher us in to that presence and give us sustenance for the journey into silence.

This book contains a selection of the hundreds of litanies I've written over the past few years. They are primarily intended for use in groups or congregations, although they certainly can be used for personal prayer practice. Typically, a leader reads the regular type, the "call," and the congregation says aloud the "response" indicated in bold type.

All of these can be used in church services and gatherings. I've tried to write prayers that help churches process and create space for issues and events, intercede together, express lament, foster joy and gratitude, build community, and ultimately as fuel for spiritual formation. My hope is that they can be used as an element of worship, but also as a formational tool. One pastor I often read is fond of saying "We are what we pray," and my hope is that these can help churches pray good prayers; stepping together into their communal Becoming, into the goodness of Christ.

I hope you'll pray them aloud together. I believe that as creatures made in the image of God, we have some of God's divine creative power: the power of Word made Flesh, of speaking hope and truth into earthly reality. So by speaking the words we form them, and ourselves, into heaven on earth. And I hope you'll get some of the benefit I've gotten from writing them, which has been an ongoing Divine Communion and twin joys of receiving and creating.

~ Fran

may your pauses be long
your silences deep
your voices sonorous
your responses resonant
and your every breath a prayer

LITANIES FOR
Looking Inward

God, we hear your invitation to us:
"Come to me, you who are weary and heavy burdened. I will give you rest."

We acknowledge our souls' need for rest and quiet nourishment.
We lay down our burdens.
We acknowledge our souls' need of connection with you.
We turn our intentions toward you now.

We confess our tendency to overlook rest
As a necessary part of soul and self care.
We confess our pride in thinking that our work is so important
That we may not set it down.
We confess our readiness to believe
That what we do determines our worth.
We confess our obsessions
With productivity, results, and measurable progress.
We confess our tendency to forget
That your love is better than life.
We confess our neglect
Of the good soil of our souls.

We ask now for body, mind, spirit, whole-person nourishment.
    For rest and resurrection,
    For new life,
    For healing and consolation of our souls.
We ask for help managing our time and activities so that our in-fillings
Can keep up with our out-pourings.

Where we have overspent ourselves
Refresh us.
Where we have misplaced our priorities
Re-arrange us.
Where we have said yes when we should have said no
Remind us.

We thank you for meaningful work; for blessings and burdens.
We thank you for rest.
May we become present to our great need for Daily Bread:
The presence of Christ in our lives.

Amen

Creator, when we walk with you,
Connected to you,
Plugged in to your love and your life,
> **Our hearts expand,**
> Our consciousness expands,
> **Our perspective expands,**
> Our reality expands,
> **Our capacity for love expands.**

We admit that we tend to become complacent
And stagnant in our imaginations.
We succumb to inertia
And allow our dreams to wither.

Awaken us now to what is inside us.
Awaken us to the authority you've given us.
Awaken us to the potential inside our situations.
Awaken us to the power we can access.

Thank you for the gifts you give us:
The talents, guidance, and purposes,
The grace, freedom, forgiveness, and mercy,
And our unique combinations of strengths and weakness.

Your love is better than life.
Your love is life.
Your highest good is beyond what we can imagine.
Help us to grow into our highest good.

Amen

Holy Spirit, Lover of our souls:
You have set us in this world,
Each with intention, destiny, and purpose,
And given us opportunities to know you,
To connect with you,
And to become our best selves.

You have given us freedom of choice on this journey.
In love you have allowed us to choose
Whether we will listen and pay attention to you;
Whether we will love you.

We choose you, our Friend and Redeemer.
Make our lives a testament to your love.
We don't want to settle for surface level
Or for a spirituality that never changes us.

Help us to be patient with the process of growth,
    To even enjoy it;
    To be present with the journey of life, spirit, soul
    To dig deep and uncover whatever is hidden
    And bring it to light (1).
    To encounter our inner shadow without fear
    To look for beauty, and do its work;
We set our intentions toward life and light.

We know that we are our best selves
When we are most aware of your grace towards us.
Walk with us on this journey of life
Now and forever.

Amen

1   Matthew 10:26

God, we are often so wrapped up in the ways we are righteous,
In defending every assault on our character.
We are preoccupied with our schedules and responsibilities
With everything we are striving to do right,
With stands we are taking
And arguments we are making.

Let us remember, as we navigate difficult times
And engage in difficult conversations,
The meekness of Christ;
Whose meekness listens quietly,
>Is not defensive,
>**Asks questions,**
>Humbly accepts correction,
>**Does not fight back,**
>Gently endures pressure,
>**Responds with love.**

Meekness lets pride fall away.
Meekness is not concerned with self-righteousness.
Meekness does not need to defend itself.
Meekness courageously embraces alert quietness.

Blessed are the meek (1).
Blessed is Christ our example,
Who is lowly, gentle, and humble of heart (2),
Who did not exalt himself (3),
Who allowed the blame of all to be put upon him
And did not protest.

Change our hearts, Oh God,
Toward meekness,
Toward the deep strength of lovingkindness,
And the confidence of your regard.

Amen

1   Matthew 5:5
2   Matthew 11:29
3   Hebrews 5:5

For this God is our God for ever and ever; God will be our guide
even to the end. (Psalm 48:14)

God, we find ourselves at a moment
When a decision must be made,
A direction must be chosen.
We seek your light and your guidance.

We desire to honor you in all that we do:
In each breath we take,
Every goal,
Every action,
Every thought,
Every interaction.

We acknowledge that our choices matter,
But that you are Author, Creator, Beginner.
We acknowledge our smallness
And our potential.
We acknowledge that we are connected to a great big world -
Parts of a body.
We acknowledge that acts of love reverberate
To all the world (1).

May all we do, and all we choose,
Be done with love;
That we may be, not a clanging cymbal or gong,
But a beautiful music filling the earth.
Help us to bravely step out onto the path of peace (2),
Trusting in your help along the way.

Amen

1   Psalm 119:64
2   Luke 1:79

in honor of Dietrich Bonhoeffer

God, we are reminded that Love is action.
As you actively love the world, we must actively love each other.
We must push past our comfort zones, reticence, and general inertia,
Allowing ourselves to be moved by the engine of Love.

We confess our tendency to withdraw.
We confess our desire to put our own safety and convenience above all.
We confess our quickness to downplay the needs of the poor,
     the plight of injustice.
We confess that we would often rather ignore the evil in our midst.
We confess that we often value our reputation above following Christ.
We confess our self-centeredness.

We ask for hearts aflame with the Love of Christ.
We ask for patience to endure suffering.
We ask for courage to pray for and love our enemies.
We ask for strength to accomplish the work of peace.

Where injustice, poverty, and wrong-doing abound,
May we do justly, love mercy, and walk humbly (1).
When laziness and complicity would overwhelm us,
May we be empowered by your spirit to renew our efforts.

We look to Christ, the model of loving sacrifice,
**And to those saints throughout the ages who have lived and died for the
     cause of Love.**
May we act with confidence and boldness,
And find our reward in the joy of your presence.

Amen

1 Micah 6:8

God, it is our nature to keep record of wrongs (1).
It is your nature to forgive (2,5).
We tend to let wounds fester.
You offer light, air, and healing.
We tend to get stuck in bitterness and pain.
You embody freedom.

Come now, into the places where our hearts have been wounded,
Where we have been betrayed or abandoned,
    Or disrespected,
    Or overlooked,
    Or kicked while we're down,
    Or stolen from,
    Or slandered,
    Or misunderstood.

Come now, into the dark parts of us that want revenge,
    That want to grind axes,
    That want our enemies to suffer,
    That want to keep a list of grievances,
    That want to prove how strong we are,
    That want to defend ourselves.
Replace our pride and bitterness
With superhuman love.

This is hard work for us:
    Becoming like you,
    Turning the other cheek,
    Making ourselves vulnerable (3).
It's why we need you so much -
Because we are weak.

We need you to move mountains for us:
Mountains of pain and resentment.

Strength, wholeness, and redemption,
Life, peace, and resurrection
Are in forgiveness;
And in forgiving, we are forgiven (4).

Amen

1   1 Cor 13:5
2   Ps 103:10-14
3   Matt 5:39
4   Matt 6:14-15
5   Ps 130:3,4

God, we know that when we wait upon you
Our strength is renewed (1).
We know that your presence can grow in us
When we become still (2).
You are exalted in our hearts
When we contemplate your goodness.

That we often avoid quiet reflection,
We confess to you, Oh God.
That we often mistake stillness for sloth,
We confess to you, Oh God.
That we often become hoodwinked by our culture of excess,
We confess to you, Oh God.
That intentional stillness often requires great effort from us,
We confess to you, Oh God.

When we are running around, attending to our to-do lists,
It's you we seek (3).
When we are looking for pleasure and consolation,
It's you we seek.
When we are in need of affirmation and success,
It's you we seek.
When we are avoiding our pain, or nursing our wounds,
It's you we seek.

We cease our striving and sink now into the stillness of this moment,
For we have composed and quieted our souls (4).
We immerse ourselves into your loving, always-available presence,
For we have composed and quieted our souls.

We make it our ambition to be deeply familiar with you,
For we have composed and quieted our souls.
We meditate upon the beauty of God,
For we have composed and quieted our souls.

Renew us now
As we wait quietly, in stillness, for you.

Amen

1   Isaiah 40:31
2   Psalm 46:10
3   Psalm 63:1
4   Psalm 131:2

God, we turn toward you now.
Be merciful to us, sinners.

We feel we must defend ourselves.
We take refuge in you.
We feel we must silence others.
We choose to be still instead.
We feel we must rebut every argument.
We look to you for what is right.
We feel we must make ourselves appear powerful.
We remember that your power is made perfect in weakness (1).

Help us to not point fingers or launch accusations.
Help us to firmly and peaceably stand up for what is good.
Help us to take care of our own hearts before criticizing others.
Help us to do justly, love mercy, and walk humbly (2).

We recognize that we are sinners
In need of mercy.
We recognize that we all see in part,
In need of divine perspective.
We recognize that we are all fighting a great battle,
In need of kindness (3).

May we imitate the humility of Christ,
Who accepted punishment,
Who endured humiliation and slander,
And used them for good.
We turn toward you now.
Be merciful to us, sinners.

Amen

1   2 Corinthians 12:9
2   Micah 6:8
3   Quote attributed to Ian McLaren: "Be kind, for everyone you meet is fighting a hard
       battle."

LITANIES FOR
Looking Outward

God of Compassion and Love,
You care for sparrows and sinners.
Your heart is bent toward the disadvantaged.
Your justice covers the rich and the beggar.

We acknowledge our difficulties in participating in your work:
Self-centeredness,
Apathy,
Disgust,
Blindness,
Pride.

These things keep us from seeing the beggar at our gate.
We need you to teach us your way.
Forgive us,
And have mercy upon us;
That we may, by having compassion, bring heaven to earth
And break down the walls of hell.

Give us courage to face the agony of those around us
And strength to help.
When we are asked to get our hands dirty, to stoop to lift the
    downtrodden,
Help us to be faithful and obedient.

Amen

God, we turn our attention now to the work of peacemaking
and reconciliation.
Christ is our peace.
We remember Jesus in the throes of death, offering forgiveness and peace
to those who had taunted and tormented him.
Christ is our example.
We remember Jesus after his resurrection, offering forgiveness and
restoration to his disciples who had denied and forsaken him.
Christ is our leader.

We acknowledge that we have wronged others and been wronged by others,
And need forgiveness applied to both.

Help us to forgive others as we have been forgiven by you,
For in forgiving, we find peace and freedom.
Help us to have humility and courage,
   To admit when we are wrong,
   To confess and apologize,
   To make amends to those we have hurt.

We acknowledge that forgiveness benefits the forgiver,
And that we can never force others to forgive us.
We acknowledge that we may never see the results of our peacemaking,
But that you see our hearts.

We thank you God, for removing our transgressions from us.
Thanks be to God.
We ask for hearts conformed to the way of Christ,
Ready to offer peace; willing to forgive and be forgiven.

Amen

God, it is into your hands that we send our Loved One.**
She* was only ever there all along.
We breathe in the peace of your presence: your presence with her*
as she sleeps
Your presence with us as we wait.

Be present to those caring for her* while we are apart.
Let the peace of your presence come to them as well.
Let your lovingkindness fill their hearts,
Calm and focus their minds; steady their hands.

Let no evil befall them or our Loved One.
May each body system come to perfect harmony.
May each wound inflicted bring health and healing behind it:
As by Christ's wounds we are healed, so now we ask for healing wounds.

Make us awake to our blessings - things we take for granted,
Things many people throughout the world don't have:
Sanitation, education, access, options, medicines and therapies;
Hope, provision, support, community.

May we care for her* with compassion and patience while she* recovers.
We know that in the midst of pain, you bring growth and goodness.
May we be strengthened and tireless as we offer help:
**Each word echoing the mercy of Christ, each action formed and
informed by love.**

Amen

** Substitute the name of the individual here
* Replace gender-specific pronouns as needed

God, you are revising our ideas about family —
Broadening them;
Helping us understand that our family lives not only within the walls
 of our own homes,
But beyond them.

As Christ has taught us
We care for little ones.
As Christ has taught us
We care for the poor.
As Christ has taught us
We care for the sick.
As Christ has taught us
We care for the imprisoned.
As Christ has taught us
We care for the lonely and orphaned.

Help us to be compassionate listeners,
Compassionate do-ers,
Compassionate helpers,
Compassionate teachers.

Help us to remember:
That it is us who are poor,
That it is us who have been lonely and sick,
That it is us whose bonds need breaking.

And as we raise up the next generation
And live as an example for them,
Let generosity and kindness be our hallmarks.
Let them know us by our love.
Let our young ones know that our arms are wide and our hearts are open
To them, and to all whom you love.

Amen

God, we lament the destruction that has been done,
That we have permitted to be done;
By our silence and inaction,
And by our direct action
To the Earth — your creation.
Forgive us, Oh God.

Even now we realize that our home
Is suffering,
Its inhabitants are suffering,
From lack of clean air and water,
Lack of life-giving nourishment,
Lack of safe habitat.

Help us to become aware
Of the needs of humanity,
Of the needs of generations to come,
Of the needs of creatures and lands.

We acknowledge that we have a chance:
To choose peace over profit,
To choose activity over complacency,
To choose a greater good over today's convenience.

Arouse in us a new compassion,
A new willingness to change,
A new excitement to foster community,
A new zeal for establishing the Peace of God,
A new understanding of the connectedness of all things,
A new appreciation of the gift of Earth.

Amen

God, we lift up to you the plight of our sisters and brothers fleeing from their homes,
Escaping war, extermination, persecution.
We pray in solidarity with those who must uproot themselves and their families in order to live.
Be with them now, Oh God.

For refugees from [Syria, Somalia, Guatemala, Iraq]* we pray:
For provision for practical needs,
For safe passage through distressed regions,
For a home, a hope, and a future.

For aid organizations and workers in those regions, we pray:
For the love of Christ to flow through them,
For world awareness and support of their needs and work;
For effectiveness in helping distressed people.

We are reminded of mandates you've given us: to extend hospitality to strangers,
To love our neighbor as ourselves.
May we live in light of your commands, and in the light of your love.
We love because you first loved us.
May we generously give, serve, and listen, sharing in the richness of the Community of God,
Extending grace and mercy to all.

Amen

* Insert the name of the country from which refugees are escaping.

God, we know that many invisible people exist all around us;
People we consider beneath us,
People we judge for what we consider their poor choices or low standards,
People we distance ourselves from because they are "unclean,"
People who have been ill or made mistakes and fallen through the cracks
of society:
The beggars at the gate.

We don't know them,
But you do.
We don't know their names,
But you know each hair on their heads.
We often fail to care for them,
But they are precious in your sight.

Help us to see what your eyes see:
Human beings,
Broken and beautiful,
Sacred and scarred.

For those without families or safety nets
We pray to God.
For those without shelter
We pray to God.
For those without jobs
We pray to God.
For those without food, water, and facilities
We pray to God.
For those who have been imprisoned and never recovered
We pray to God.

For those whose minds are befuddled by illness
We pray to God.
For those destroyed by war
We pray to God.
For those governed by addiction
We pray to God.
For those who have simply lost hope
We pray to God.

In the midst of death and dying,
Of dirt and discomfort;
Of hunger, thirst, and exposure,
Come Lord Jesus!
Make us your hands and feet:
Generous sharers and helpers,
Bearers of the good news of your kingdom -
Even unto the invisibles.

Amen

God, this life here on earth is a mixed bag
Of joy and pain,
Grief and exuberance,
Stillness and frenzy.

We don't get to choose where we are born, or to whom,
But we know you made us and we are your children.

Open our eyes to all the ways we are blessed,
That we may share and bless others.
Open our eyes to all the ways we have been born to privilege,
That we may live with grateful hearts.

In many ways we are born to pain.
Let us bear one another's burdens.
In many ways we are born weak and blind.
Let us be kind to one another.
In many ways we are born to poverty.
Let us know the riches of your grace.

May we spread goodness and mercy wherever we go,
Regardless of where we come from.
May we find healing and acceptance with you
And know you as the one who gives good gifts.

Amen

God, who so graciously speaks to us and is present to us,
Help us to be present to you, and to your people.

We confess that we have avoided quieting ourselves before you.
We confess that we are distracted and noisy people.
We confess that we are often so busy speaking that all we hear is
       our own opinions.
We confess that we've been afraid of what you might say to us.

We turn now to you, knowing that you are love, and that love is what you
       are always telling us, even when you are gently correcting us.
We need gentle correction now.

We confess that we have not listened to our neighbors.
**We confess that we have not made time and space to hear their stories
       and concerns.**
We confess that we have allowed our differences to put us off.
We confess that by not engaging, we have stifled love.

Show us how to open our ears and hearts to those of different cultures,
       races, backgrounds, belief systems.
Show us how to love our neighbors.
Show us how to embody the mission of Christ: to prepare a great banquet
       and invite everyone to feast.
May we know your voice.
May we make space in our lives to hear your voice and do your
       good work.
May we follow the promptings of your Spirit without hesitation.
May we overcome our fears of shame, and our reluctance to experience
       awkward moments.
May we live love loudly, and listen quietly.

Amen

God, we seek your wisdom for how to live today, in this time and place.
We ask help from you:
>   To remember that we are citizens of heaven first and foremost (1) -
>   **Help us, oh God;**
>   To live with integrity and fidelity to Christ even while under
>   human government -
>   **Help us, oh God;**
>   To practice peace and resurrection in our every action (2)-
>   **Help us, oh God;**
>   To exercise our rights and privileges on behalf of the vulnerable -
>   **We need the mind of Christ.**

We lift up those human leaders in authority,
That they may do justly, love mercy, and walk humbly (3);
That they may overcome self-interest with self-sacrifice;
That they may listen to the voices of the people they serve;
That they may have vision for good for all, beyond partisan goals
    and nationalism;
That they may resist temptation to wield their power for personal gain;
That they may resist tyranny, totalitarianism, and autocracy within
    their ranks;
That they may speak truth, and uphold it (4);
That they may hold fast to laws which foster justice, and root out those that
    discriminate against the weak;
That they may seek peace and pursue it (4);
That they may work for equality and benefit for all races, all genders, all
    religious and cultural expressions;
That they may champion the beauty of humanity from cradle to grave;
That they may regard kindness and cooperation as strengths;
That they may lead with humility, morality, compassion, and creativity.

Let everything that is hidden come to light -
The light that is Christ. (5)
And let all people live in the authority of the Kingdom of Heaven,
Under the law of Love.

Amen

1   Philippians 3:20
2   "Practice resurrection" is a line in Wendell Berry's famous poem
    "The Mad Farmer Liberation Front"
3   Micah 6:8
4   Psalm 34:14
5   John 8:12

God, you have made people of every imaginable kind:
Colors and shapes,
Privileged and marginalized,
Rich and poor.

We have differences of every imaginable kind:
Perspectives and worldviews,
Countries and cultures,
Philosophies and theologies.

We acknowledge that we tend to fear what we don't understand,
And that love is more powerful than fear.
We acknowledge that we must work to understand each other,
And that this work is Kingdom work.
We acknowledge that each perspective brings your nature into
     clearer picture,
And that we need each other's points of view.

Help us to love one another
Even though we are different.
Help us to celebrate one another
Even though we may not agree.
Help us to be kind to one another
Even when we have been hurt.
Help us to open the doors to our churches,
     Homes,
     Organizations,
     Governing bodies,
     Dinner tables,

Even though it may feel awkward and impractical.
We know that the diversity of the people of the world is a good gift,
For our growth and edification;
To help us see your vision for the world:
> **Where there are neither slave nor free,**
> Male nor female,
> **One race nor the other;**
But we are all free, beloved, and united
In the peace of Christ Jesus.

Amen

After reading the story of Shiphrah and Puah in Exodus 1

God, you have saved us by many creative means
Over the years of humanity's existence.

You've saved your people by means of trumpets and shouts,
    By means of manna from heaven,
    By means of water from rocks,
    By means of the miraculous and the mundane.
And you've saved your people by means of valiant midwives:
Those women entrusted to usher the future into the world
In the midst of pain and travail,
With wisdom, experience, and alertness.

May we all be like the midwives,
Working in quiet devotion
Or in subversive creativity —
Those who care for those who carry,
Those who shift breaches and unblock exits,
Those who comfort and calm,
Those who urge us to PUSH when the time is right,
Those who know when to wait and when to cut,
Those who catch slippery bundles of goodness as they emerge,
Those who bind up wounds of effort.

May we have the vision of the midwives
Who could imagine a future beyond what they could see,
And were willing to risk their lives and reputations
To give it a chance to arrive.

We thank you for the Midwives,
For those who are as shrewd as serpents,
As innocent as doves (1),
Protecting the future as it is born.

Amen

    1   Matthew 10:16

Oh God, we are reminded today of your infinite love for all people:
All races
All colors
All political affiliations
All religious persuasions
All social classes
All economic statuses
All nations.

We confess our tendency to think that we are the best, our perspective
the most righteous.
Forgive us our arrogance, Oh God.
We confess our tendency to judge others, and to condemn those we
find unworthy.
Forgive us our presumption, Oh God.

We see others with criticism.
You see us all with love-filled eyes.
We see only in part.
You see the world with infinite wisdom.
We see the external.
You see the heart.

Mold us to your way.
Form us to your heart.
Shape us with love.
Make us new with grace.

Our way is not of violence and empire, but in the power and beauty of the cross.
Our faith is not in politics, but in the transforming love of Christ.

May we work diligently to help meet the needs of those you love, both
physical and spiritual.
May our eyes be opened to the value and worth of each person we meet.
May your kingdom come, your will be done
On earth as it is in heaven.

Amen

God, make us attuned to your compassion,
To the kindness of your heart.
Transform our hearts and minds so that in kindness
We weep with those who weep.
In kindness,
We rejoice with those who rejoice.

So that in kindness
We listen to the stories of others.
In kindness
We regard them as more important than our own.
In kindness
We allow ourselves to see hidden broken hearts.
In kindness
We perceive a greater story.

In kindness
We care for the orphan and the lonely.
In kindness
We care for the sick and the prisoner.
In kindness
**We care for those whose lives are just beginning and those whose lives
are at an end.**
In kindness
We care for those in crisis and in need of refuge.
In kindness
We care for those disregarded, disempowered, and marginalized.

In kindness
We consider how to maintain our hope.
In kindness
We consider how to serve our communities.
In kindness
We consider money and power as tools for good - not end-goals.
In kindness
We consider all humans to be made in your image.

May the precious kindness of Christ,
Which firmly corrected and firmly forgave;
The precious kindness of Christ,
Which prevailed over death, violence, and empire;
Guide our hearts and voices
And keep us in perfect peace.

Amen

LITANIES FOR

Coping

God, our hearts are weary,
Broken, and sad.
Grief follows us;
Pain is our companion on the road.

We are divided: parents against children,
Brother against brother
Sister against sister,
Half-nation against half-nation.

The sins of our past have revisited us.
They were just beneath the surface,
Covered in a coat of whitewash.
We are newly aware of our complicity.

We mourn our blindness.
We regret our apathy.
We weep at the state of our world.
We wish we had done things differently.
We grieve the wrongs done by us and by others
And reap a harvest of shame.

We open our hearts before you;
We are vulnerable and at your mercy.
Let your will be done to us.
Refine us in your fire.

We purpose ourselves now to walk steadfastly and humbly
Through the chafing grief
And the ache of suffering,
Out to where the mercy falls (1).

Amen

1   "Where the Mercy Falls" is the title of a song by David Ruis and Bob Hartry

God, we are thankful
For those who have survived,
For those who have helped and responded,
For what spaces are left to rebuild in,
For the people who embody love,
For experiences that teach us what matters.

We acknowledge that those beset by disaster have endured great trauma:
The losses and mess,
The danger and fright,
The distress to body and soul.
These are deep wounds, real wounds
That take time to recover from.

You weep, oh God, with those who weep.
You mourn with those who mourn.

Heal your people, oh God.
Rescue them from their distress,
Enfold them in your kindness,
And surround them in your care.

Make of us a strong and resilient people:
A people prone to compassion,
A people prone to good works,
A people prone to patience,
A people prone to listening,
A people healed and whole.

Let the work of rebuilding —
Lives, homes, livelihoods, communities —
Be the work of new life and imagination;
The work of Heaven-on-Earth.

Amen

God, many of us have been hurt
By those who should have cared for us.
The Good News has become skewed,
Used as a tool,
Used to manipulate,
Used as a weapon.

Some of us have left the faith
Rather than continue to be hurt.
Some of us have carried our wounds
Into our present lives and communities.
Some of us have been silenced.
Some of us have been told that we are too much,
    Not enough,
    The wrong gender,
    The wrong orientation,
    The wrong race.
Some of us have been told that we've misheard our callings.
Some of us have been rejected altogether.

We acknowledge our pain
And need of your healing.

Where our spirits are atrophied from disuse,
Heal us, oh God.
Where our wounds have left deep scars,
Heal us, oh God.
Where our hearts are shut down and hardened,
Heal us, oh God.
Where we have silenced our souls,
Heal us, oh God.
Where we have let unforgiveness fester,
Heal us, oh God.

Let the pattern of abuse and trauma end with us.
Let us live out love openly and unapologetically.
Let our lives be informed by the life of Christ,
And Christ be the seed of our imagination in this life.

Amen

God, we cry out to you on behalf of the people of [Orlando]*.
For the families and friends of those killed in the attacks, we cry.
For those wounded, we cry.
For the bystanders, those shocked and terrified, we cry.
For the emergency workers, giving tirelessly of themselves, we cry.
For those in government and law enforcement, we cry.
For the residents of the city, stranded and immobilized, we cry.
For a world beset by evil, we cry.

We commend the souls lost into your care,
And ask for healing and comfort for those that remain.

These events bring us into a place of questioning:
Of your goodness,
Of your sovereignty,
Of the nature of humanity,
Of the future of the world.

We commend those questions into your care,
Asking you for wisdom,
Asking you for hope,
Asking you for courage to continue on in good work,
Asking you for help in overcoming,
Asking you for comfort in trouble,
Asking you for a heart of love toward our enemies,
Asking you for justice.

We acknowledge that our lives are precious, vulnerable, and often short.
We acknowledge that safety is never guaranteed.
We acknowledge our inability to perfectly follow Jesus' example of
        meekness and peacemaking.
We acknowledge that when Jesus took upon himself the wrongdoing
        of the world, he took terrorism also.

We look toward the fullness of your kingdom come, your will done
    on earth as it is in heaven.
We look toward the completion of Jesus' work.

We look toward and the day when the whole world is aligned with the
    law of love.
Be near to the brokenhearted,
Close in your compassion and lovingkindness,
Generous in your giving of understanding.

Amen

* Insert the name of the city you are praying for today.

Note: this litany was originally written after the Orlando nightclub shooting of June 2016.

God, things are changing.
The world is changing.
We feel uncertain and shaky.
We feel anxious.

Questions have arisen that we've never had to deal with before.
Give us wisdom.
Shifts in culture and technology have brought problems we've never
   had to face before.
Give us discernment.

We are divided in our opinions of how to move forward.
We want unity.
We disagree on policy.
We want compassion.

We know that the Kingdom that Christ began on earth
Is progressing.
The good news
Is expanding;
The momentum of your will being done on earth as it is in heaven
Is unstoppable.

Even as all around us changes,
Your love endures forever.
Even in war, and climate change, and social media,
Your love endures forever.
Even in theological and political disagreement,
Your love endures forever.

Help us to love one another as never before -
Better than before.
Help us to not be defensive or closed-minded,
But open to the Kingdom coming in unexpected ways.

Amen

God, help us to remain calm in troubled waters,
When things to fear are real or imagined.

When we are tested (1),
Help us to endure.
When we are criticized,
Help us to endure.
When we are misunderstood,
Help us to endure.
When we miss the mark,
Help us to endure.
When things are loud around us,
Help us to endure.
When peace seems impossible,
Help us to endure.
When common ground feels like compromise,
Help us to endure.
When we are thwarted,
Help us to endure.
When discouragement seems like the only reasonable response.
Help us to endure.
When we are tempted to prepare our defense (1),
Help us to endure.
When those we love feel like enemies,
Help us to endure.
When our enemies are hard to love,
Help us to endure.

We know that we gain our souls
By quiet, uncomplaining endurance.
We know that endurance
Expands our souls.

In all things,
May we have the mind of Christ.

Amen

Here is a litany that is a meditation on loss and a prayer for grace and comfort in the experience of it. Feel free to choose the reference words (things, people) to suit your situation. In the case of the loss of an animal you might use "friend."

God of comfort, restorer of all things,
We look to you in times of trouble.
Something (someone) has been lost
Which (whom) we held dear.
We feel emptiness and sadness at this loss.
Comfort us with your presence.

We understand that within the confines of time,
All things must end.
We understand the cycles of life and the seasons -
Still we find the changes painful.
We acknowledge that we feel entitled to keep things (people)
By virtue of having been given them,
And that we feel affronted and angry when the time of our
    keeping runs out.
Give us grace to be grateful for the gifts of life, however long we get them.

We accept the gifts you give,
And the potential for pain they arrive with.
We understand that holding tightly to a thing (person)
Is sometimes not the best way to love it (him, her).

We are reminded that you hold all life within your gracious love.
You are gathering all things to yourself (1).
You have power over death, are author of life, and are first to resurrection.
We trust you to care for what we have lost.

Help us as we stumble around
Overwhelmed by pain;
And in our human experience, during which loss is inevitable,
Help us to see the divine.

Amen

1   Ephesians 1:9-10. I really like Eugene Peterson's MSG translation of this.

God, some of us are bombarded with messages that tell us we should
   never feel sad,
That we should ignore pain or cover it up.

Some of us are bombarded with messages that tell us we should
   only feel sad,
That we should give up hope altogether.

We are grateful for your balanced view,
And for your example
Of acknowledging people's pain and darkness,
And companionably entering into it with them;
Of letting death think it won for a hot minute
Then BOOM: resurrection!

Death overcome!
Grief turned to joy!
Weeping turned to laughter!
Pain and travail: a child is born!

Help us to live as faithful Grievers
Of whatever anguish we encounter or experience,
Who are willing to walk among despair.
And help us to live as faithful Hopers,
Courageous people of good cheer
Who are certain of our impending joy.

Amen

Oh God, our hearts are overwhelmed with sorrow for the endless trauma
that continues to afflict the people of the earth.
Our hearts cry out.
We lament the violent tragedies that have occurred in recent days both at
home and abroad.
Our hearts cry out.

We lift up our eyes to the hills;
Where will our help come from?
Our help comes from the Lord
Who made heaven and earth (1).

Violence, murder, trauma, chaos - they seem to be unending and
gaining momentum.
How long must we wait, Oh Lord?
Governments overrun, children and families killed, tension and
fear rampant.
How long, Oh Lord?

We have nothing left but to hope in you, God.
Our hope is in you.
Our grieved hearts have nowhere else to turn.
Come quickly to rescue us.

We pray for peace.
Yes.
We pray for violence to end.
Yes.
We pray for your merciful heart to beat inside us.
Yes.
We pray for you to show us how to help.
Yes.

We are pressed on every side,
But not crushed;
We are perplexed,
But not in despair;
We are persecuted,
But not abandoned;
We are struck down,
But not destroyed.
Death is at work in the world,
But life is at work in you.

Come now and bring life.
Our hope is in you.

Amen

1   From Psalm 121
2   From 2 Corinthians 4

God, we hold our lives loosely before you,
Offering them up to you.
You have asked us to trust in you.
We trust in you.
You have asked us to be loyal to you.
We give you our loyalty.

Everything we have - every relationship, every possession –
Is nothing compared to the richness of your kingdom.
Everything required of us in following you
Is nothing compared to the joy of your presence.

Help us to get our priorities straight,
To honor you with everything we own, and everything we relinquish.
We entrust you with the people we love
Understanding that your love is greater.

Help us to become willing
To follow you,
To endure whatever suffering we must encounter,
To humble ourselves,
To let go of things that hold us back,
To risk our security,
To embrace awkwardness,
To go all-out for love.

When we are tempted to let ourselves be motivated by comfort –
To hide behind apathy –
Re-orient us to your Kingdom and your love.
Correct us, and be our shepherd.

May we faithfully follow the example of Christ,
And live in his light.

Amen

(From reading Luke 18)

God, our faithful Friend:
We know that you are not like the unjust judge in the parable.
You are just and merciful and compassionate.
We often find it difficult to hold suffering in our minds alongside hope.
Our hearts are often fragile
And our minds forgetful.

Help us to be ok with expressing a full range of emotions:
Lament and joy,
Anger and affection,
Gratitude and disgust,
Excitement and sadness,
Doubt and empathy.

Help us to be disciplined, grounded in practices that bring us life:
Prayer,
Meditation,
Fasting,
Sabbath-rest,
Worship.

Grant us a river of hope
That flows beneath all we do,
In which we may refresh ourselves
Whenever we grow weary.

And help us to be as persistent as the widow:
Not losing hope,
Praying without ceasing,
Seeking and working for justice.

Amen

Oh God, we remember now Christ in his suffering, and echo the feeling in
His words: "My God, my God, why have you forsaken me?" We remember:
You are with us.
We remember Christ tempted in the desert, Christ suffering at
Gethsemane, Christ hung on a cross.
You are with us.
We see that suffering echoed in our own lives, and acknowledge our
inability to suffer as Christ did, perfectly, without sin. We remember:
You are with us.

When we are uncertain,
You are with us.
When we have lost things or people precious to us,
You are with us.
When sickness overtakes us,
You are with us.
When we are overwhelmed with grief,
You are with us.
When we are exhausted from our labors,
You are with us.
When enemies rise up against us,
You are with us.
When our souls are in the dark night,
You are with us.

We take comfort in Christ, who is a man of sorrows, acquainted with grief; and
we are consoled by his having walked the road of suffering ahead of us.
You are with us.
We believe anew in the resurrection of Christ from the dead.
You are with us.

It is because of Christ that hope still stirs within us.
You are with us.
And it is by his example that we turn to you in the midst of our suffering.
You are with us.

May our dry bones be enlivened; our stone hearts be made flesh; and our
    sickness be not unto death.
You are with us. Hallelujah.

Amen.

LITANIES FOR
Church Rituals

This litany is intended to be used in times of baby/child dedication or welcoming a new child into the community.

God, we thank you for the gift of this/these* child(ren).
And for his/her/their* parents.

We know that you have entrusted them to their parents
And also to our community;
To care for them,
To teach them,
To be examples of Christ's compassion to them,
To inspire them.

Because we know that we can't protect them from every possibility of pain,
We ask you to keep them safe.
We commend them to your care,
Knowing that you pour out love on all people.

Help us to provide them with everything they need to become strong:
Physical and spiritual nourishment,
Stability and freedom,
Boundaries and opportunities,
Wisdom and encouragement,
And above all: love.

We know that raising kids is hard-but-holy work.
Give patience to us all, God.
We ask that, in response to your kindness to us,
We are able to offer them kindness;
And thus to grow the world's capacity for kindness,
In raising kind humans.

Bless these children,
And let us be a blessing to them.

Amen

* Change all pronouns to suit the people you're praying for.

God, you bless us in all kinds of ways.
The sacraments you offer us are blessed.
You are always teaching us who we are
By your gifts, presence, and words to us.

For the baptism with water, a symbol of our new life,
We give thanks.
For baptism of your spirit, the gift of your presence in and among us,
We give thanks.
We accept these gifts as a sign of your love and regard,
As a sign of you being with us.
As symbols of your promises to us:
You cleanse, fill, and renew us.

With living water
We are washed and filled.
With holy spirit
We are washed and filled.

You come to us with the beauty and gentleness of a dove:
We are your children, in whom you are pleased (1).
And you come to us with the intensity of a fire:
We are your servants, to do your work in the world.

Fill us anew each day
With water and fire.
Teach us to walk as New Creation,
New creatures, children of God:
Buried with Christ in death
Raised to newness of life (2).

Amen

1   Mark 1:10,11
2   Romans 6:4

God, we lift our pastor(s)* up to you now
Asking for peace,
Asking for help,
Asking for wisdom,
Asking for protection,
Asking for renewal.

We know that they often bear heavy burdens,
Knowing the burdens of many.
We know that they often work long hours,
Sacrificing for the good of their community.

As they sit in the secret place,
Visit them.
As they discern difficult situations and deal with difficult people,
Go with them.
As they care for the sick, hurting, imprisoned, and stubborn,
Care for them.
As they live out their callings and exercise their giftings,
Walk with them.
As they confront their own inner shadow,
Enlighten them.
As they encounter temptation,
Keep hold of them.
As they encounter evil,
Deliver them.

May they know that here, among us, is a place they are welcome -
Their true selves,
Broken, scarred, redeemed, learning, growing alongside us,
Moving always closer to the heart of Christ.
May they have hearts of gratitude and joy,
Finding fulfillment in their work.
May they seek and find the Divine,
And help us to find you also.

Amen

* Feel free to substitute "priests" or "ministers" in place of pastors as per your tradition. Also feel free to substitute masculine or feminine pronouns in place of they/them.

God, we welcome these folks* into our midst,
Into community with us.
We thank you for their presence here
And willingness to join in our work.
Grant that we may be caring, supportive, prayerful, and intentional friends,
Working together for their good.

Grant that they may find us to be a community of peace,
A community of love,
A community of thoughtfulness,
A community of generosity.

Grant that they may find among us deep friendships,
Soul renewal,
Spiritual nourishment,
And inspiration to grow.

Be always and ever present with them,
That they may find meaningful work,
Walk in their giftings and callings,
Be encouraged in their relationships,
Practice prayer and presence,
And be continually called toward Christ.

Let us be a healthy community:
Serving one another,
Giving to those in need,
Following the Way of Christ.

Bless our friends, oh God,
And let us be a blessing to them.

Amen

*   Insert the names of the people or family being welcomed

God our Creator,
God our Teacher,
God our Friend,
God our Love:

We are hungry for your goodness
And thirsty for Living Water.

We set our intentions toward improving our skills,
Growing our spirits;
Enlarging our body of knowledge,
Growing our abilities;
Enhancing our servant leadership,
Growing our understanding;
Strengthening our communities,
Growing our capacity to love.

Let music flow through our bodies
And praise bubble up on our lips.
Let humility be what we're known for
And worship be our daily rhythm.
Let the love of Christ be our means and our ends
And your presence be the true home of our hearts.

Giver of wisdom, helper and guide:
We look to you.
Creator, Son, and Spirit:
We wait for you.

Amen

God, we are grateful for each member
Of our Beloved Community (1).
Here, there is no Us or Them,
Only We,
Only All,
Only Welcome.

Empower each of us to find our place
    In the Family,
    In the network of community,
    In the work.
Grant that we may know ourselves well,
Our giftings and callings,
And that we may know each other well,
Encouraging each other to thrive.

There is no greater;
There is no least.
There are no glorified tasks;
There are no meaningless tasks.

Give to those who volunteer their time, effort, and resources,
Rest and renewal,
Support and connection,
Purpose and energy,
Satisfaction and encouragement,
Joy and fulfillment.

For each person who joins in the work that we do,
We thank you.
For each person who contributes as they are able,
We thank you.
For each person who puts the weight of their effort into the work of Justice,
We thank you.
For each person who must, at various times, rest and receive the
    community's love,
We thank you.

And may each volunteer be blessed with every spiritual blessing
In Christ Jesus (2).

Amen

1   The "Beloved Community" is a reference to the ideas and preaching of
    Dr. Martin Luther King Jr.

2   Ephesians 1:3

God, we are grateful for the gift of {name of person seeking ordination}
For her* dedication to ministry,
For her love and service to the community,
For her willingness to work among your people.

We stand alongside her and affirm
That she is called to ministry,
That she is gifted for ministry,
That she is passionate for your community,
That she is doing the necessary inner work to reach spiritual maturity,
That her life bears fruit in keeping with repentance (1),
That she is committed to the Way of Christ,
That the light of Christ burns brightly within her.

We bless her now
To love and serve you,
To be filled with your spirit,
To study, contemplate, and receive wisdom,
To be constantly renewed in love,
To walk in a manner worthy of Christ (2),
To produce the fruit of good work,
To increase in the knowledge of God (2).

Grant that she may serve you faithfully,
Helping to bring heaven to earth.
Grant that she may receive support
From family, community, and the Holy Spirit.
Grant that she will be blessed,
With the abundance of heaven.

And at the end of a long life of service and walking with you, may she be received by you with these words:
"Well done, good and faithful servant" (3).

Amen

1   Luke 3:8
2   Colossians 1:10
3   Matthew 25:21
*   Substitute the appropriate pronouns

God, we remember the Lord Jesus on the night he was betrayed. He took
bread, broke it and said:
This is my body, broken for you.
And in the same way he took the cup, saying:
This is my blood, shed for you (1).

We proclaim the Lord's death until he comes again (2).
He was pierced for our transgressions,
He was bruised for our iniquities,
By his stripes we are healed (3).

We proclaim that we do not live on bread alone, but by the
Word Made Flesh (4):
Jesus, the Bread of Life (5).
The daily presence of Jesus in our lives is our sustenance,
Jesus, the Living Water (6).

We take this bread and cup in communion with our brothers and sisters
In remembrance of Christ (1).
Christ, the Word of God, spoken to us; Christ, alive and present with us...
Christ, our daily bread (7).

Amen

1   Luke 22:19, 20 ; 1 Corinthians 11:24, 25
2   1 Corinthians 11:26
3   Isaiah 53:5
4   Matthew 4:4, John 1:14
5   John 6:35
6   John 4:14
7   Matthew 6:11

Oh God, we are reminded that you are the author of work, rest, and play.
Hallelujah.
We recognize our being made in your image, having need of all three.
Hallelujah.
With consciousness and intention, we now set aside our daily tasks and
    make space for relaxation, revival, and enjoyment.
Hallelujah.
We breathe deeply of your presence, and drink deeply of your delight.
Hallelujah.
We pray for open ears and soft hearts, that we might hear your renewed
    calling on our lives and be willing to accept it.
Hallelujah.
We soak in the freedom and joy of being among people who share
    in our passions.
Hallelujah.
May we emerge from our respite with clean hands, pure hearts, and
    steadfast spirits.
Hallelujah.

At the end of our rest, may we re-enter our ministries with refreshed
    balance, purpose, energy, and clarity.
Hallelujah.

Amen

God, we know that death is not a change to be feared,
But a transition to be honored.
We have this pattern:
Death, burial, life
Repeated throughout nature
And re-imagined by Christ.

We sow in death.
We reap in life.

We do not fear death
Because Christ has conquered it;
Christ, the first fruit of those who have died (1),
Is resurrecting us alongside himself.

Therefore we do not lose hope.
Instead we revel in life:
Abundant,
Everlasting,
Increasing,
Transforming.

We come awake to the cycles of life and death,
Knowing this is right and good,
Befriending beginnings and endings,
Remembering that death is a doorway.
And, in spite of pain or grief,
In spite of a perception of loss,

We are certain that Christ is waiting for us
On the other side of death.

Be with us, oh God,
Now and at the hour of our death.

Amen

1   1 Cor 15:20

LITANIES FOR
Communal Worship

Is anything too wonderful for the Lord (1)?
Nothing is too wonderful for you.
You make wonders bloom from your hands,
And from your imagination spring amazing things.

Your wonders will never cease.
Your wonders will never cease.

Old women bear children (2).
Trees bear fruit out of season.
Rocks give forth springs of water (3).
Seas part (4).
Storms are stilled (5).
Sickness and disease are cured (6).
Whole nations are brought out of bondage (7).
Crowds are fed from your hand (8).
Dry bones are enlivened (9).
The dead are raised to life (10).

Your wonders will never cease.
Your wonders will never cease.

We enter your presence with thanksgiving,
And your courts with praise.
We give thanks to you,
We bless your name.
For you are good; your steadfast love endures forever,
And your faithfulness to all generations (11).

Amen

1	Genesis 18:14	7	Exodus 20
2	Genesis 21:2	8	Matthew 14, 15, John 6, Mark 8
3	Numbers 20:11	9	Ezekiel 37
4	Exodus 14:21	10	John 11, Mark 5, Luke 8, 1 Kings 17, 2 Kings 4, and many more
5	Matthew 8, Mark 4		
6	Matthew 10:8	11	Psalm 100:4,5

Oh, the majesty and magnificence of your presence!
Oh, the beauty of your sanctuary (1)!

Give to the Lord honor and offerings
For great are you, Lord, and greatly to be praised (2).
Give to the Lord glory and honor -
The glory and honor due to your name (3)!

We enter your gates with thanksgiving, and your courts with praise (4).
To be in your presence, Lord, is joy.

Where the Spirit of the Lord is, there is freedom (5).
To be in your presence, Lord, is to be free.
You bless your people with peace (6).
In your presence is peace that surpasses our understanding (7)

We earnestly seek the presence of the Lord all day long.
Joy, freedom, and peace are the hallmarks of our lives.

Daily we carry the presence of the Lord with us,
And this mystery is Christ in us, the hope of glory (8).
Daily we acknowledge Christ, in all things;
For in him all things hold together (9).

Daily we reach out for you, Lord, and find you, for you are not far from us.
In you we live and move and have our being. We are your children (10).

Amen

1) Psalm 96:6	6) Psalm 29:11
2) Psalm 96:4	7) Philippians 4:7
3) Psalm 96:7	8) Colossians 1:27
4) Psalm 100:4	9)Colossians 1:17
5) 2 Corinthians 3:17	10) Acts 17:28

God, it was your voice, the vibration of your words, that set the first
molecules into formation and motion.
You sang the universe into being.
Your breath first nudged planets and atmospheres into existence, by the
rasp and melody of your speaking.
You sang the world into being
Like the cascade of waterfalls, the rumble of thunder, the whir of wind, and the
soft breath of infants - so is the beauty and power of the voice of our God.
You sang creation to life.
You moved air through lungs of dust and called us Beautiful, named us
Beloved, and shared with us your energy and your art.
You sang humanity to life.

When we say that we live and move and have our being in you, God, we
mean that from wave to particle to atom to molecule to cell to organ
to body - you are within and throughout.
Your voice makes us.
You are Love, and Love set the earth spinning and the stars shining and
our hearts beating.
Your voice makes us.
Love that sings and vibrates, dances and gyrates; Love that never stops
being and becoming.
Your voice makes us.
Love that energizes and ennervates, uplifts and invigorates; Love that
multiplies and amplifies.
Your voice makes us.

In Christ, Love put on a human face; took on vocal cord, consonant,
resonance, and sustain.
Hallelujah!
In Christ, Love decided that dying was dancing and resurrecting was to
be expected.
Hallelujah!

In Christ, Love said that loss is gain and death is life and power is weakness and dissonance is harmony, and then proved it.

Hallelujah!

In Christ, Love is re-making every broken thing; every off-key note and accidental, every counterpoint, coda, and hum is arranged to beauty.

Hallelujah!

In Christ, Love is singing again, and still singing: a song of redemption, invitation, and new creation.

Hallelujah!

Amen

God of peace and love, bring to us a new awareness
Of your kingdom at work in the world.
Grant that we may see and understand
The small and unassuming things,
Which take patience and attention to notice:
>**A seed,**
>Yeast in bread,
>**Treasure buried in a field,**
>A net cast into water,
>**A baby lying in a manger.**

We acknowledge that we mostly miss the signs when they are not flashy or
earth-shaking,
But that your kingdom is all around us.
We acknowledge that Christ came to exhibit neither wealth nor
political power,
**But self-sacrificing love, which the world had never seen and
mostly overlooks.**
We acknowledge that the progress of the good work we do may be
imperceptible to us,
And that our success is in our obedience to you.

We welcome your kingdom, in the world and in our hearts.
We seek your kingdom, certain that we will find it.

We anticipate your kingdom,
>**Working toward peace,**
>Providing for the poor,
>**Healing the sick,**
>Loving our enemies.

We trust in your love to provide for us in our seeking.

Whether your spirit comes to us as a wind or a whisper,
May we know your presence and be useful to your kingdom work.

Amen

Ruler of heaven and earth:
We exalt you!
We come into your presence with singing and thanksgiving (1),
Because you are good!
You have reached out to us with open arms.
Your love endures forever (2)!

Heaven and earth are yours, created by you.
We belong to you!
Your beauty and power astound us.
We want to see your glory!
For you are above all things and before all things,
In you all things hold together (3)!

Everything in the world that distracts and tempts us
Is nothing compared to you!
Everything that would keep us from your love,
You have overcome!
Everything we need
You have provided!

We want to be in your presence always, every minute, every day.
We worship you, and you only.

Amen

1) Psalm 100:4
2) Psalm 136:1
3) Colossians 1:17

Great God, you created the good earth and all its creatures, the heavens
and all they contain.
We give thanks.
You created us to be in community with you, and to please you.
We give thanks.
You give us life. You give us consciousness. You give us love.
We give thanks.

For the blessings of family, friendships, and worldly provision,
We give thanks.
For the blessings of talent, aptitude, and meaningful work,
We give thanks.
For the blessings of food, drink, and good conversation - those times of
feast and enjoyment,
We give thanks.
For the blessings of trivial pleasures, small gifts meant for our happiness,
We give thanks.
For the blessings of expression, song, art, human ingenuity, and creativity,
We give thanks.
For the blessings of peace that come from knowing you,
We give thanks.

When we survive mishaps,
We give thanks.
When we endure consequences and pain,
We give thanks.
When we must combat evil with goodness and love,
We give thanks.
When we must deny ourselves, bear burdens, and obey,
We give thanks.

When we must suffer loss and disappointment,
We give thanks.
When me must come to the end of our physical lives,
We give thanks.

When we chose violence and rebellion, you made a way to recover us.
We give thanks.
The way of Christ, the true and full, shining image of your love.
We give thanks.
For Jesus Christ and the Kingdom he began here, in which you invite us
to participate,
We give thanks.
And for the experience of living on earth, in all its paradoxes and
mingling of joy and suffering,
We give thanks.

Amen

God, it is you who made us.
We belong to you.
You created every detail of our beings.
We belong to you.

You are unimaginable in every way. Our best guesses about you don't come
    close to your glory.
We belong to you.
You have blessed us immensely: with your presence, with love, with Christ
    and the Spirit
We belong to you.
You have made us one with you in Christ (1)
We belong to you.

We often go around thinking that we are separate from you -
Separate from each other -
But the truth is that we are all made of the same dust (2)
Parts of the same whole.

Oh God, grant that we may know the vastness of your love,
The depths of our belonging.
And grant that we may live in unity
With one another, and with you.

May we live each day, resting in this welcoming truth:
We belong to you.

Amen

1   Galatians 3:28
2   Ecclesiastes 3:20, Genesis 3:19

God, we have come here together
To draw near to you.
In community and in expectation
We draw near to you.

To be at one with you, in your presence,
Is our greatest gift.
To sit at your feet, absorbing your love,
Is our greatest blessing.

You have made yourself available to us.
We draw near.
You have opened the heavens to us.
We draw near.
You have given us the keys to the kingdom.
We draw near.
You have shown us the path of peace.
We draw near.
You have brought us into your family.
We draw near.

Let every corner of our hearts
Be open to you.
Let every hidden attitude
Be open to you.
Let every life's story
Be open to you.
Let every unseen ending
Be open to you.

The best life we can imagine
Is lived close to you.
To be wholly present to you is our desire.
We draw near to you.

Amen

God, this is who we hold up high,
This is who we look to:

To Christ, who exceeded every expectation,
Defied every convention,
Fulfilled every prediction,
Revealed every intention.

Christ, who irritated the rule-makers,
Upstaged the Sabbath-breakers,
Out-played the money-schemers,
Inspired the justice-bringers.

Christ, who blessed the merciful,
Praised the peacemakers,
Empowered the healers,
Embraced the outsiders.

Christ who forgave the unforgivable,
Loved the unlovable,
Redeemed the unredeemable,
Touched the untouchable.

Christ, who endured suffering,
Faced down death,
Emptied the grave,
Raised up life.

Christ, light in darkness,
Peace in storm,
Comfort in trouble,
Strength in weakness.

Christ, whom God embodied,
Whose image is Divine,
Whose heart is pure,
Whose love we share.

Christ, who was, and is, and is to come,
Who walked, preached, healed,
Who was crucified, died, and buried.
Christ has died. Christ is risen. Christ will come again.

Amen

God, we know that you are in community - with Creator, Christ, and Spirit
And with us.

We know that we need each other and you to thrive
> **To survive,**
> To share burdens,
> **To share joys.**

We know that you made us to learn in community
> **With each other,**
> From each other,
> **For each other.**

As your Trinity is in perfect, loving community,
So make us into a community of perfect love;
Which banishes fear,
Which encourages faith,
Which offers nourishment,
Which values kindness,
Which includes and liberates,
Which inspires and creates.

We know that when we irritate or hurt each other,
We are learning.
When we have conflict,
We are learning.
When we dialogue and listen,
We are learning.
When we forgive and reconcile,
We are learning.

We know that what annoys us about others,
Is probably a projection of ourselves.
We know that humility is our best attribute,
And earth is a school of forgiveness*.

So, commune with us now,
Oh, Great Community.
Teach us your ways,
Teach us how to live in love.

Amen

> * This is referencing Anne Lamott, who said, "I really believe that earth is forgiveness school – I really believe that's why they brought us here, and then left us without any owner's manual. I think we're here to learn forgiveness." From a Facebook post on Dec 2, 2014.

Surely goodness and mercy will follow me all the days of my life, and I will dwell in the house of the Lord forever. (Psalm 23:6)

God of goodness and mercy: we admit that we have gotten off-track.
We know we need to do justly,
Love mercy,
Walk humbly (1).

We are enticed by retribution
And take vengeance for ourselves (2).
We are enamored by damnation
And forget about goodness.
We are in love with judgement
And disregard mercy.
We need a change of heart.
Christ, have mercy on us.
We need to look into your eyes and have our inner world transformed
Before we begin work on the world around us (3).

Transform and renew us now (4)
Into the image of Christ,
Into a peace-making people,
Into a just and merciful people.

May we scatter seeds of goodness and mercy wherever we go,
And live in the light of your presence always (5).

Amen

1   Micah 6:8
2   Romans 12:19
3   Matthew 7:3
4   Romans 12:2
5   Psalm 23.6

Injustice

This litany has been one of the most-shared, most-widely used that I've written. As events have occurred across the country, bringing to light deep wounds and scars of racism left by slavery, genocide, and hatred; many congregations have looked for ways to address racism aloud together, pray together, and work toward healing in their communities. I offer this option.

Oh God, visit us now in our mourning,
Be near to us in our lament.
Blood has been shed, precious lives have been lost, evil has had its say.
Christ, have mercy.

We acknowledge the hold racism and prejudice have on our
        national psyche.
Set us free from this bondage.
We acknowledge that violence has been matched with violence, and
        many are in pain and distress.
Bring healing to us all.

We pray now for the Church in America, part of the body of Christ on
earth, that it may be a voice of peace,
A light of love,
Working for reconciliation and unity,
Working for justice.

We stand in solidarity with our brothers and sisters, all races, all skin
        colors, all ethnicities.
Hallelujah.
We stand against racism and injustice.
Hallelujah.
We stand for love.
Hallelujah.

For all the ways we are complicit in perpetuating racism,
Forgive us, Oh God.
For all the ways we have hidden the light of Christ,
Forgive us, Oh God.

For all the times we have kept silent,
Forgive us, Oh God.
For all the times we have capitulated to fear of ridicule and retaliation,
Forgive us, Oh God.
For all the ways we've given over to apathy,
Forgive us, Oh God.
For all the ways our own prosperity has blinded us to the needs of others,
Forgive us, Oh God.

Protect the innocent Oh God!
Hallelujah!
Open the eyes of the blind!
Hallelujah!
Rout out the unjust!
Hallelujah!
Thwart the plans of the greedy and power-hungry!
Hallelujah!

May Christ, who re-imagined death, give us inspiration for how to
move forward.
Love triumphs over hate.
May Christ, who said upon rising from the grave, "Peace be with you,"
bring us into his kingdom.
Peace triumphs over violence.
May Christ, who did not retaliate but offered forgiveness, share with us
his vision.
Mercy triumphs over judgement.

Amen

If you're using this litany in a congregational or group setting, I recommend omitting the "We acknowledge" section. For the purpose of personal prayer, I feel that section contains worthwhile reminders about Jesus and his ideas about power.

God, our hearts are hurting for our sisters and brothers who have been
   victims of rape, sexual abuse, violence.
Help us to help and care for them, and stand in solidarity with them.
For those who are victims of sexual violence we pray.
Lord, have mercy.
For those whose bodies and minds have been violated,
Christ, have mercy.
For those who have been overpowered physically or emotionally,
Be their refuge.
For those who have felt helpless,
Be their stronghold and help in trouble.
For those who have borne up under sexual abuse,
Be their comfort and healer.
For those who have felt too damaged in body or mind to go on,
Be their hope.
For those whom the legal system has failed,
Fight for them, Oh God.

We acknowledge that violence is not the way of Jesus.
We acknowledge that Jesus never forces his way on us, but wins us.
We acknowledge that Christ awaits our consent to enter our hearts
   and lives.
**We acknowledge that Christ loved and respected people from all walks
   of life, all genders.**
We acknowledge that Christ did not wield physical power over people,
   but healed and forgave.
We acknowledge that justice belongs to you, and we can trust you for it.
We acknowledge that Christ came to save the world;
   The victim and the perpetrator,
   The rich and the underprivileged,
   The foolish and the wise.

God, hear our prayer:

We ask for justice,

Understanding that we may not see it this side of eternity.

We ask for peace,

Which the Spirit of God is always offering here and now.

We ask for mercy,

For violence to cease.

We ask for rest,

That those traumatized may sleep each night in the peace of your presence.

We ask for redemption,

For the perpetrators to repent and make amends.

We ask for healing,

For deep wounds to be mended.

We ask for forgiveness,

That victims may be free from seeking revenge, and perpetrators may be made new by the forgiveness of Christ.

May your kingdom come on earth.

May your love abound to all, redeeming all.

Amen

Advent

God: as the light of day fades in the evening
We hope for the sunrise.
As leaves journey toward earth mulch
We hope for good soil.
As the winter deepens around us, hollowing to sleep
We hope for springtime.
As all around us sleep the sleep of the wrecked
We hope for healing.

We wait in wakefulness,
Eyes open,
In readiness and expectation,
For you to come;
For you to call us on a journey —
We wait awake.

On the dawn
Goodness comes.
With green shoots
Goodness comes.
From earliest darkness
Goodness comes.
From darkest soil
Goodness comes...

The Goodness that is dung and straw and lamb and shepherd and angel -
Our God-With-Us;
The Goodness that is fresh babe -
Our Holy One;
The Goodness that is Messiah -
Our humble king.

Amen

God, we are longing for a silent night —
For a reprieve
From noise and anxiety and hurry;
For a moment
Of space and time, empty yet full.
Gift us the gift of quiet.

This is the peace:
Of baby's breath,
Of feathered wing,
Of rustling leaf,
Of sphere's turn,
Of light beam.

The heavenly peace in which we long to rest,
To sweetly sleep
In safety and freedom,
In certainty and repose.

We can smell the peace
Coming on the wind.
We can feel the peace
Arriving with the morning.
We can taste the peace
In the bread and cup.

We look in your direction, God
The Place from which peace comes;
For you are its author and the home of its Prince,
And in your peace we dwell.

Amen

God, all kinds of feelings pass through us in this life:
From happiness to sorrow and everything in between.
We can look around and see all kinds of reasons not to feel joyful
Until we learn:
Joy is not felt
Joy is found.

We straighten our spines,
Posturing ourselves toward joy;
Needing constant rediscovery
Until it becomes our nature.

Joy in pain,
Joy in transformation,
Joy in journeying,
Joy in growth,
Joy in parting,
Joy in waiting.

This is the joy that wells up from us:
The intentional song,
The thoughtful gift,
The word of comfort,
The broken thing mended,
The belly filled.

This is the joy given to us:
To love and be loved,
To sacrifice and be blessed,
To be lost and found.

Joyful, Joyful!
Rejoice, Rejoice!

Amen

God, in the waiting and the tension
You are teaching us
The characteristics of True Love.
Like a prism, it has many faces:
>Patience,
>**Courage,**
>Gentleness,
>**Honesty,**
>Kindness,
>**Freedom.**

For years, for generations, we said
"God is Love,"
When what we really thought was
"God is wrath."
We thought of you as moody and prickly,
Distant and disembodied.

We know better now.
The Christ has taught us.

We like to imagine the night Love became incarnate:
>**Clear,**
>Still,
>**Peaceful;**
Perfect conditions for Love's emergence
Perfect timing for Love's expansion.

It's in quiet that Love has its purest voice.
It's in stillness that Love finds its rhythm.

And indeed, Love smiled upon us that day,
Its every face beaming:
A tiny voice bawling out Love's insistence;
A tiny heart beating out Love's cadence.

Shhh, we can still hear it:
I love you. I love. I am Love.

Amen

God, we can wait our whole lives for it to look like Christmas.
We can rely on tinsel and twinkle lights,
We can conjure up nostalgia with cookies,
We can spray cans of snow on trees,
We can fill stockings with miscellany.
We think we can buy Christmas.

But this is what real Christmas looks like:
Mother laboring in a barn;
Babe in manger, sticky from birth;
Stink of cattle, dung, and hay.
Starlight shining on crisp plains;
Exhaustion, and milk-drunk sleep.

And the lingering question:
What do we do now?
Now that the world has become quiet,
Now that everything is changed,
Now that we have seen a Great Light,
Now that we have Wonder?

Christmas is sweaty work,
And joyful,
A long push,
And glorious,
Traveler's grit,
And graceful.

Christmas is subtle things reverberating,
Past, present, future re-made.
Christmas is small things making meaning,
Hopeful waiting and arrival.
Christmas is homeless finding refuge.
That is the Gloria the angels sing.

Amen

Lent

Holy God: in this season of Lenten fasting we remember Christ
Who went out into the desert to fast and undergo temptation (1).
We confess that we are often distracted by material comforts
And tempted to value them above the Kingdom of God.

You, God, are our help in difficulty.
Christ is our inspiration.
We confess that we do not live by bread or worldly provision alone,
But by every word that comes from your mouth (2).

May we fill our mouths, our hearts, our minds now with your words,
That we might be transformed and renewed.
May we, with renewed hearts and minds,
Better serve the purposes of your kingdom.
May we, by setting aside worldly distractions
Become more like Christ.
May we, with purified motives and deeper understanding,
Receive Christ when he comes to us.

Lead us not into temptation,
But deliver us from evil.

Amen

1   Matthew 4:1
2   Matthew 4:4

Hear, Oh God, when we call to you.
Have mercy on us and answer us.

In our vulnerability
Have mercy on us, oh God.
In our forgetfulness
Have mercy on us, oh God.
In our anxiety
Have mercy on us, oh God.
In our wrongdoing
Have mercy on us, oh God.
In our hard-heartedness
Have mercy on us, oh God.
In our blindness,
Have mercy on us, oh God.

In your mercy you rescue us from our enemies.
In your mercy you remove our transgressions from us.
In your mercy you reconcile us to you.
In your mercy you sent the Christ to heal our brokenness.

Grant that in this season of Lent, our hearts may be devoted to you,
That we may see your mercies new each day (1).
Grant that we may be always ready to offer mercy to those in need of it,
For mercy triumphs over judgement (2).

Amen

1   Lamentations 3:22
2   James 2:13

God, in this season of Lenten fasting we set our eyes toward you.
We turn our hearts in your direction.
We acknowledge our great need for you, and our great hunger.
Give us food from your hand, oh God.
We confess that we often seek to fill a void inside us with frivolous things, spiritual junk food.
Forgive us, and bless us with manna from heaven.

We set aside the expectation that our hunger might be satisfied by anything but your Spirit.
Nourish our souls, oh God.
We rely upon your promise of provision.
They that hunger for righteousness will be filled (1).
Where we are empty
Fill us up, oh God.

Jesus said: "I am the bread of Life. Those who come to me will not hunger" (2).
We come to you, Jesus.
We do not live by bread alone
But by every word that proceeds from the mouth of God (3).

Amen

1   Matthew 5:6
2   John 6:35
3   Matthew 4:4

God, in this season of Lent we reflect upon our emptiness, and
  your fullness.
Our souls thirst for you.
We come to you, Wellspring of Life.
Our flesh longs for you.
You graciously offer us a fountain of water, springing up to eternal life
In a dry and weary land, where there is no water (1).

Jesus, you are the Living Water, the holy spring
You satisfy our deepest needs.
Whoever drinks of the water you give
Need never thirst again (2).

We acknowledge the miracle, mystery, and kindness of your provision
We were thirsty, and you gave us a drink.
Fulfill now your promises to us:
That those who thirst for righteousness will be filled (3).

May our hunger, thirst, and need always lead us to you
Let all who are thirsty come to Christ and drink.

Amen

1   Psalm 63:1
2   John 4:14
3   Matthew 5:6

God, in this season of Lent
We quiet our souls (1),
That we may see more clearly the one our hearts long for.
We ask, seek, and knock (2),
That our prayers may be answered
And our longing fulfilled.

We acknowledge that so much of faith-life involves waiting,
> **For the voice of God to speak,**
> For the Spirit of God to move,
> **For the fullness of your kingdom to come,**
> For Christ's appearance on earth,
> **For the world to be made new,**
> For justice and peace to become ordinary,
> **For love to become the world's motivation.**

We acknowledge that even as we wait, you are working:
> **Redeeming the earth,**
> Redeeming people,
> **Making all things new.**

As Christ waited three days in a tomb,
So do we wait for resurrection life.
We wait in faith,
That you are even now giving us new life.
We wait in hope for the Lord.
All creation waits for the Lord (3).

Amen

1   Psalm 131:2
2   Matthew 7:7-8
3   Romans 8:19

Hosanna!
Blessed is he who comes in the name of the Lord (1)!

The One we have long awaited, the Messiah, has come.
Hosanna!
Riding into Jerusalem, not on a warhorse, but on a young donkey,
Hosanna!
The Prince of Peace has come, the one who heals our wounds.
Hosanna!

Everything that was foretold, Christ has fulfilled.
We offer a sacrifice of praise and thanksgiving.
We set up a banquet, and pour costly perfume at his feet (2).
Blessed is he who comes in the name of the Lord.

This is Jesus,
Whose name is glorified.
This is Jesus,
High and lifted up.

Hosanna!
Blessed is he who comes in the name of the Lord!

Amen

1   John 12:13, Matthew 21:9
2   John 12:3

Great God, we acknowledge that we are not always able to recognize your ways as good.
We confess that we are, at times, confounded;
As on Good Friday, when we commemorate the death of one so dear to us:
The Savior, Christ the King.

As a seed must pass through death to sprout new life,
So Jesus Christ has passed into death.
Taking the nature of a human, a servant,
He made himself nothing.
He humbled himself by becoming obedient to death,
Even death on a cross (1)!

For three days, we wait with him, for death to accomplish its purpose;
For Christ's sacrifice to be made meaningful;
For Christ to re-imagine death.
We grieve, even while we are hopeful.

We wait, and as the stones seal Christ's body in the tomb, even then we say:
"Oh Death, where is your sting? O Grave, where is your victory?" (2)
And we acknowledge your good way, the confounding way of obedience to death
That brings us toward life and hope.

Amen

1   Philippians 2:8
2   1 Cor 15:55

God, your works are marvelous,
Your power, amazing.

We are astonished at what you have done:
You have raised Jesus,
Who was put to death at the hands of an angry multitude,
Who was beaten, nailed, and pierced;
You have raised him to glorious life.
We are astonished at this gospel.

We stand now silent before you, too surprised for words.
(pause)

And now we raise a shout:
(All:) HALLELUJAH!

That Jesus Christ, put to death on a cross
Is now alive and ruler of the world!
Again we raise our voices:
(All:) HALLELUJAH!

For death has lost its sting.
The grave has been overtaken by life.
The new kingdom has begun.
The way of love is victorious.
And this gospel fills our hearts, and all the earth:
(All:) Christ has died. Christ is risen. Christ will come again.

Hallelujah!

God, we lift up to you the courageous souls who go against the grain of
the present age:
The Heretics;
The ones who flout religious tradition or expectation:
The Brave;
The ones who offend the powers and principalities:
The Prophets;
The ones who see past the acceptable and into the excellent:
The Beloved;
The ones who do the Kingdom work despite resistance:
The Committed;
The ones who sacrifice possessions and reputations for good:
The Sold-Out;
The ones who speak truth to power:
The Bold.

May their faith never falter,
Their feet never stumble,
Their resources never run out,
Their hope never die.

Because they are the ones we need
To shake us up and inspire us.
They are the ones we need to become:
The stout-hearted, beautiful Heretics;
The voice crying in the wilderness,
"Prepare the way of the Lord" (1).

May the beauty of the Good News,
The Way of God breaking in,
So stir and astound and awaken us
That we can't help but join them.

Amen

1   Isaiah 40:3

ACKNOWLEDGEMENTS

Many thanks to my readers, patrons, and friends who support my work. And deep, deep gratitude to my life partner, Jordan, who typeset and designed the artwork for this book; and who has been gradually awakening with me day by day, all these years.

Rev. Fran Pratt is Pastor of Worship & Liturgy at Peace of Christ Church in Round Rock, TX, where she lives with her spouse and two daughters. More of her work can be found at www.franpratt.com.

Made in the USA
Monee, IL
03 March 2021

61804142R00080